INK ON PAPER

INK ON PAPER

selected and edited by Colette Bryce

First published 2008
by Mudfog Press & mima

Mudfog Press
c/o Arts Development, The Stables, Stewart Park,
The Grove, Marton, Middlesbrough TS7 8AR
www.mudfog.co.uk

mima
Middlesbrough Institute of Modern Art
Centre Square
Middlesbrough
TS1 2AZ
www.visitmima.com

Copyright of introduction and poems © the authors
All art works published with the kind permission of the artist unless otherwise stated save where these could not be found or contacted.
All rights reserved

Edited by Colette Bryce for Mudfog

Cover design by turnbull.fineart@virgin.net

Print by EPW Print & Design Ltd., Middlesbrough. Tel: (01642) 231055

ISBN   978-1-899503-76-6

Mudfog and mima gratefully acknowledge the support of Arts Council England, Middlesbrough Council and the Tees Valley Writers and Publishers Project.

As a gallery professional, one spends a great deal of time considering the reactions and responses that exhibitions or exhibits stir in the viewer. Though galleries are much more attuned to pursuing feedback and monitoring audiences these days, I have always believed that an important part of an individual's engagement with an artwork is a matter for personal contemplation. Beyond that, an articulation of it would be too complex and too delicate to reshape into something that a statistician could meaningfully use to access trends. Within the pages that follow, however, I suspect the creative manifestation of such feelings and ideas has found the perfect home. At the same moment, the undeniable creativity that has been poured into this collection of poetry will now go on to inspire new reactions in another audience and perhaps these readers will be brought back to the original artwork and source of inspiration, thus closing the circle. Beyond that, I feel sure these words and thoughts will enrich the way in which readers of this collection will look at all visual art in the future.

I would like to thank and congratulate all those who have contributed their creativity to this project, not least Colette Bryce and Paul Batchelor. Thanks are also due to Sandra Reddie of New Writing North, several members of Mudfog Press and Nina Byrne for coordinating the delivery of the project and, lastly, to the artists whose work inspired the writers, who I hope will inspire you, the reader.

Godfrey Worsdale
Director
Middlesbrough Institute of Modern Art

The Tees Valley Writers & Publishers Project worked together with Mudfog Press and mima to form a new creative partnership. Together we developed a project, which offered an interesting opportunity for Tees Valley writers. Poets Colette Bryce and Paul Batchelor were tasked to select inspiring items from the 2007 mima collection exhibition and to lead four writing workshops at mima. These summer workshops, described as 'excellent', 'inspirational' and 'stimulating' were the catalyst for the poems included in this collection. We are delighted that the project has culminated in such an innovative anthology and aspire to develop further mutual opportunities for creative projects in the future.

Sandra Reddie
Tees Valley Writers & Publishers Project

Funding Note
The Tees Valley Writers & Publishers Project is hosted by New Writing North, the writing development agency for the north east region and supported by Arts Council England North East, Darlington, Hartlepool, Middlesbrough, Redcar & Cleveland and Stockton-on-Tees Borough Councils, the European Union via the Arts Council's Cultural Sector Development Initiative and the Tees Valley Investment Fund.

This book is dedicated to the memory
of three fine local teachers - one artist, two poets -
who inspired many
with their love for and talent in their particular art

Pat Brown
John Carter
Kath Finn

Introduction

Sometimes a painting will summon an emotion that takes us, the viewer, completely by surprise. Or our curiosity might be aroused by the story suggested in a composition. A certain sculpture can inexplicably connect us up with a childhood memory. We enter that space between image and language, where our own particular experience enriches our ways of seeing, sensing, responding – of being in relationship with art.

The ancient tradition of Ekphrasis, where one artistic medium relates directly to another, has always attracted poets. The word comes from the Greek *ek* and *phrasis*, 'out' and 'speak', the verb form meaning to proclaim or call an inanimate object by name. Some of the most loved poems in English were created in relationship with art. One thinks of Auden on Breughel's Icarus, or Keats' Ode on a Grecian Urn. A browse through contemporary poetry collections will often reveal a poem or two in response to visual art.

So the idea of inviting local writers to the new Middlesbrough Institute of Modern Art, in order to engage creatively with the exhibits, was a welcome one for all concerned. The poets, both published and unpublished, spent hours wandering through the galleries, opening their minds, looking, discussing, thinking and writing. In workshops with the poet Paul Batchelor and myself, they experimented with various approaches and ideas and started the poems that eventually came to be written up and collected here.

There are poems about, poems to and poems from the point of view of the artworks and their subjects. Others take the image as a starting point only and lead us off on an imaginative journey. They invite the reader to listen in to the age-old conversation between poetry and art, and to look afresh at the selected works from mima's remarkable collection. We hope you enjoy them.

Colette Bryce
Newcastle, October 2007

Table of Contents

Poem Bowl – Rupert Spira
The Curve of a Pig's Back – Jo Colley, *Page 15*
Jane – Adrienne Silcock, *Page 17*

Tracy Emin – It Never Felt Like This
Screwed – Katie Metcalfe, *Page 21*
Illusion – Katie Metcalfe, *Page 22*
A Son – Pat Borthwick, *Page 23*

Conrad Atkinson – Wall Street Journal 27/50
Picasso Lashes Thatcher Proposals
for Education and Employment – Annie Wright, *Page 27*
Dream Headlines – Sheila Nichols, *Page 28*
Vermeer to Attend Salt Talks – Diane Cockburn, *Page 30*

Ivon Hitchens – Green Glade
Green Glade – Pauline Plummer, *Page 35*
Salad Days – Monica Sharp, *Page 36*
Green Glade Sounds – Maureen Almond, *Page 37*

Jeff Luke – 9-5 Part II
The De-Generation Game – Natalie Boxall, *Page 41*
Christmas Day – Carmen Thompson, *Page 42*

Ceal Floyer – Ink on Paper
Ink on Paper – Geoff Strange, *Page 47*
Setting Out Our Stall – Diane Cockburn, *Page 48*

L.S. Lowry – The Old Town Hall and St Hildas Church
The Old Town Hall – Geoff Strange, *Page 53*
The Old Town Hall and St Hilda's Church – Keith Porritt, *Page 54*
Ex Cathedra – Norah Hill, *Page 55*

Ian Macdonald – Broken Nose
Blooding the Enemy – Marilyn Longstaff, *Page 59*
You Should've Seen the Other Fellow – Ann O'Neil, *Page 61*

Richard Slee – Chicken Legs
Chicken Legs 2005 – Gordon Hodgeon, *Page 65*
Chuckalishas – Katie Metcalfe, *Page 67*

Frank Auerbach - Seated Figure
Seated Figure – Monica Sharp, *Page 71*
Chair – Pat Borthwick, *Page 72*
Auerbach's Figure – Anne Hine, *Page 73*

Henri Gaudier-Brzeska – Wrestlers
The Wrestling – Pauline Plummer, *Page 77*
Wrestlers – Joseph S. Kelley, *Page 78*
Getting There in Spite Of – Jo Heather, *Page 79*

Colin Pearson – Large Winged Vessel
Large Winged Vessel – Jon Glasper, *Page 83*
Large Winged Vessel – Gordon Hodgeon, *Page 84*
The One – Jo Heather, *Page 85*

Edward Burra – The Market
Don' Mek Me – Annie Wright, *Page 89*
The Capital of Cabbage-Land – Joanna Boulter, *Page 91*
Don't You Find – Marilyn Longstaff, *Page 92*

Rupert Spira

Poem Bowl, 2006

Thrown stoneware bowl, poem inscribed through black pigment over white glaze
© Rupert Spira

Photography Gilmar Ribeiro, g2
Acquired through the Northern Rock Foundation Craft Acquisition Fund

The Curve of a Pig's Back

I am hungry
the poem bowl is empty
I am thirsty
the poem bowl is dry

soak the poem bowl in water
for forty days and forty nights
remain vigilant
on the 41st day at dawn
check the bowl
read the poem

I am hungry
the poem bowl is empty
I am thirsty
the poem bowl is dry

hold the poem bowl over a gentle heat
(wear asbestos gloves)
remain vigilant
after several minutes
(this may vary: more for epics
less for haiku)
check the bowl
read the poem

I am hungry
the poem bowl is empty
I am thirsty
the poem bowl is dry

take a photograph of the bowl
enter a dark room
develop the photograph
as it floats in its warm bath of chemicals
check the bowl
read the poem

I am hungry
the poem bowl is empty
I am thirsty
the poem bowl is dry

sit on a street corner on an old blanket
place the poem bowl before you
ask passers-by for spare poems
at the end of the day
check the bowl
read the poem

I am hungry
the poem bowl is empty
I am thirsty
the poem bowl is dry

gaze at the bowl as if it were
the face of your lover
admire its curves
the intricacy of its surface
your fingers itch to learn
allow the poem to appear
read the poem.

Jo Colley

Jane

a million words inscribed
inside Jane's head
imbecilities, wisdoms
the bizarre, the mundane
lines that could cover
an earthenware bowl
highlight grace, beauty
instil serenity

but these words won't emerge
they catch in her throat like dry toast
choke her, steal her breath
drink the moisture from her tongue
until it swells and clamps her jaw

and when they ask her
why don't you talk, why don't you say how you feel
she has no answer –
her shoulders squeeze a shrug
her eyes hunt for escape
and she yearns to spread her words
from top to centre in calm curves
light settling upon them

Adrienne Silcock

Tracey Emin
It Never Felt Like This, 1999

Monoprint
Courtesy of White Cube, London
© *Tracey Emin*

Photography Gilmar Ribeiro, g2
Presented by the Contemporary Art Society, 2003, purchased with a grant from Arts Council England with funding from the National Lottery

IT NEVER FELT LIKE THIS

YES YOU DID

AND YOU KNEW
IT WOULD
FEEL
LIKE
HELL

Screwed

I'm screwed.
I lost you.
Atop my pyramid
I am
But you're trailing.
I'm clinging
Balking yet praying I won't fall
And lose more
Of this emotional core
The scrap that remains.
Hanging loose, noose-like
Over the tub
My buttocks pale and protruding,
Breasts all askew,
One leather boot
Full of the remnants of you,
The other still
There, only just
But so?
I can't ride down the tiled mountainside,
I haven't, as yet, cleaned up.

Katie Metcalfe

Illusion

Hurt like hell at the beginning,
He promised passion then you
Hell, right – did he shite
No goddamn hero that night.
So I'm sorry,
Your entrance
Wasn't really that nice
And your exit was worse.
Someone will be inspired
Yet you can never be sure.
Warped how some minds work,
Critics always stab and backlash
Then spoon out a million from air
For an illusion on tiles
Not hay.
Wonder if my fuckup,
My sweetheart, my darling
Will end up that way.

Katie Metcalfe

A Son

You'd have been a young man now,
even your imperfections perfect. I've seen you
dipping under arches down the Cam,
your tall reflection among upturned fiery trees

and not a single drip from your quant pole.
At ten, you taught yourself to cook Thai;
simple blossoms in red-glazed vases
set to the exact geographic East of our plates.

Do you remember when you were six,
how you poured warm oil in a tjanting
then showed me how to bathe Toby's eyes
before he trundled into hibernation?

From your pram you could hollow a pumpkin
and carve any expression in it.
The candle's amber flame
chuckled on the gatepost all night. Blackberries.

Our hands are still stained and clotted. That too
was in October. You are especially in October,
October the twenty-eighth, a Thursday,
the day I had to use my overnight case.

Can we get you anything? the nurses asked,
with their eyes hidden in their pockets.

Pat Borthwick

Conrad Atkinson

Wall Street Journal 27/50, 1985

Lithograph
© *Conrad Atkinson*

Photography Gilmar Ribeiro, g2
Acquisition supported by the V&A Purchase Grant Fund

THE WALL STREET JOURNAL.
CHIEFS OF STAFF
MICHELANGELO QUESTIONS U.N. PRIORITIES ON FAMINE RELIEF AND CASH CROPPING IN THIRD WORLD
REMBRANDT
in call for trade sanctions against South Africa.
RAPID EXPANSION WOULD WORRY ME SAYS CEZANNE
NANCY REAGAN AND BERTHE MORISOT DISAGREE ON BASIC PRINCIPLES OF COLOUR AND COMPOSITION
PICASSO LASHES THATCHER PROPOSALS FOR EDUCATION AND UNEMPLOYMENT
Pentagon turns down strategic defence initiative by Velasquez
Nudity
KINNOCK AND RAPHAEL IN BUST-UP ABOUT THE MEANING OF BEAUTY
VERMEER TO ATTEND SALT TALKS.
DA VINCI HUSTLES N.A.S.A. ON GENERAL PHILOSOPHICAL PRINCIPLES
MARKET STATISTICS
Veronese argues that Brunelleschi design for new Pentagon is prime example of cultural appropriation
Reagan tax plan at odds with the Divine Spirit alleges William Blake
Pentagon Plans To Boost Beauty, Reduce Clearances
MATTISSE SAYS THATCHERISM FAILS TO RECOGNISE PLEASURE PRINCIPAL
Fra Angelico utterly opposed to star wars defines the plan as unethical, unworkable, ungodly.
"Call me a sentimental aesthete, old formalist if you like but I like to see a nicely painted missile" — tender boneless chicken chief argues national heritage enhanced by beautiful missiles
IBM and third world representatives discuss the complexity of meaning in the inverted figures of Baselitz
Let's get personal
Dow Jones & Company, Inc. invites you to a seminar on Dow Jones Art /Retrieval
A demonstration and training session for our online cultural service
GOYA to appear before grand jury
27/50

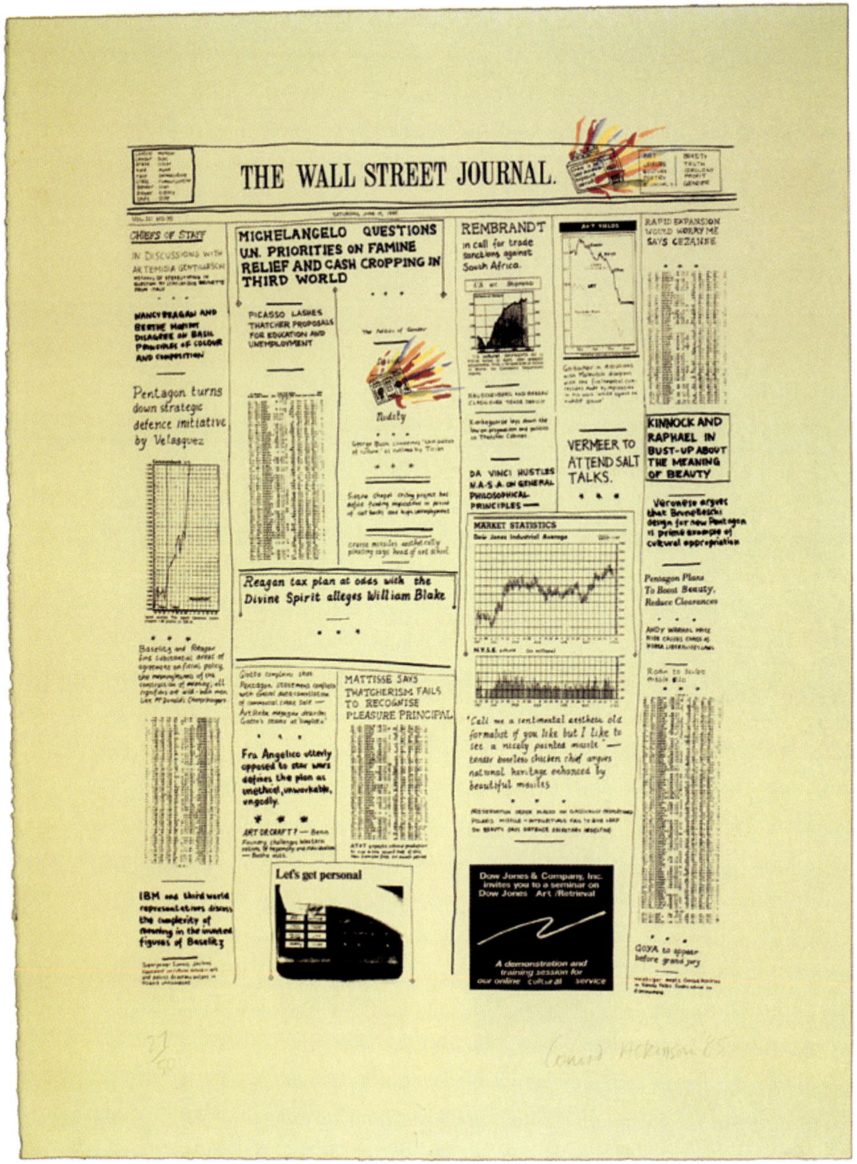

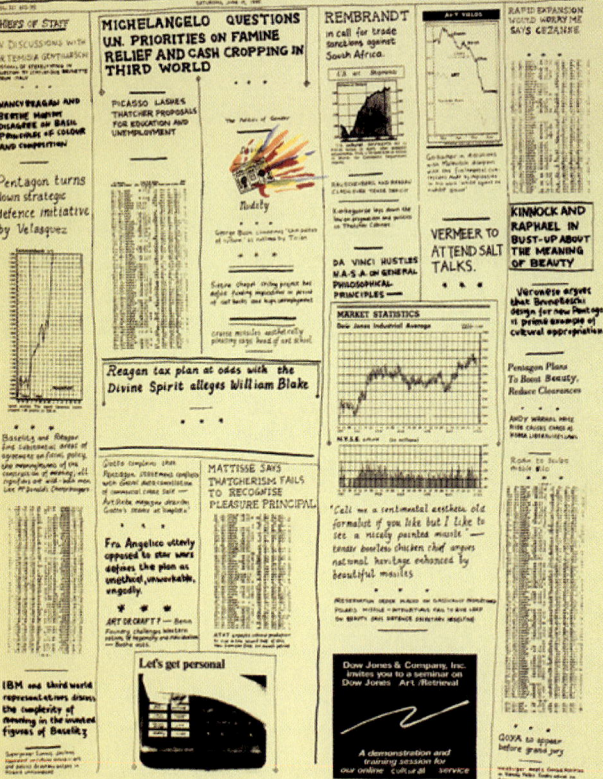

Picasso Lashes
**Thatcher Proposals
for Education and Employment**

Picasso locked horns with Thatcher yesterday as his posthumous portrait *Cat with nine tails, two heads and infinite possibility* was unveiled at Tate Modern. Artist Pablo (109), snorting and stamping, lashed out at government proposals to cut unemployment at a stroke by requiring the jobless to sign up for University.

Accusing his recent work of lacking balls, the Iron Lady set out her stall: *Any fool can get an Art degree, stop scrounging and become a decorator*. The Spanish bull saw red: *Has she never heard of Hitler? Madam, any mad cow can run a country but no artist worth the name would waste his art here or give you a tinker's fart!*

Annie Wright

Dream Headlines

Michelangelo unhappy at
feminist allegation of glass ceiling.

MOD and Da Vinci deadlocked re
nuclear sun and WMDs

Matisse says Kyoto No Go

Stock Market slump likely, says Rodin

Sister Wendy to attend Star Wars seminar

RSPCA and NSPCC join forces
to attack Damien Hirst; 'Out of his skull'
says Hieronymous Bosch

Cherie Blair and Renoir at loggerheads
over property deal

Putin criticises Van Gogh's use of colour –
'Not enough red!'

'Small is beautiful' brigade protest outside
David Hockney exhibition

Rembrandt blows cold on wind farms
Mugabe goes head to head with Rousseau
on crop rotation

Manet challenges Soho call girls to debate
principles of Form and Motion

Afghan poppy lord in bed with Slumberland
in marketing campaign

Global Poverty Summit needs to join dots,
says Miro

'Call me a torch bearer for 21st Century women'
says Tracy Emin – 'You may think so,
I couldn't possibly comment,' says Grandma Moses

Sheila Nichols

Vermeer to Attend Salt Talks

Bit of a bugger really.
There we were, all ready to have big important talks,
about salt, mainly.
In comes Vermeer, pencil behind his ear.
Sits down, starts to sketch the proceedings.
We voted for the casual grouping, with tasteful headgear;
he wanted the light just so, something domestic, he said,
with grapes. Oh, and someone with a big bust turning just so, to
catch the viewer's eye. Big on the whole rolled up sleeve; had a bit of a thing for it,
if you ask me. I won't mention the neck ogling.
Well, my skin's like an old codpiece, so I was out of the running and I've never
played the lute.
Then he starts demanding kitchen utensils and discreet ewers!
That was it. I jokingly asked for the cruet, seeing these were salt talks.
He throws a wobbler, squeezes a yellow paint tube into the mayor's ear and insists
we wear ridiculous hats. Red furry I can live with. Purple beret a definite no.
Jan by this time decided enough was enough and opened the meeting with salty
anecdotes.
Piet twanged something on the virginal and lisped a shanty.
I opened the salt sack ready for tasting.
Well, that was it.
The salt. The evening. The full moon.
Didn't think to mention to Vermeer we met late afternoons.
Forgot to remark upon the way the golden light suddenly dips away in that corner of
the house.
Perhaps should have asked how he felt about salt itself.
Everything happened at once.

Mrs Jensen slipped on a linseed oil slick, crashed into the salt sack.
Salt sack split; burst open over Vermeer who was stooping to twitch a drapery.
Moon came out; he gave a strangled yelp and began to bubble
all over his red velvet smock.
Dropped to his knees, face went all sucky and eyes popped out on stalks,
back twisted into hard horn spiral, pantaloons exploded,
goo everywhere, smell of mushrooms.
We all screamed. The mayor's wife was enveloped in slime. Last thing I saw of her
was a dissolved breast and one blue satin slipper.
Piet screamed 'Were-snail!' and crossed himself in salt.
Vermeer trailed slowly towards the door, sucking demands for
dog poo down payments.
Didn't stand a chance when he hit the pavement.
Exploded in a kaleidoscope of pigment.
Gritters had been out.
Be advised, citizen, when you plan salt talks,
always include a desiccation clause.

Diane Cockburn

Ivon Hitchens
Green Glade, 1961

Oil on canvas
© *Estate of Ivon Hitchens*

Photography Gilmar Ribeiro, g2

Green Glade

Green is on a wavelength of 500 nanometers
which must shift so slightly
for these nine shades of green
olive, avocado, eau-de-nil, bottle, pea
lime, pistachio, jade, emerald.
Did the painter try to mix
the exact shade the Koran
calls the colour of paradise
or the secret shade of the heart chakra
or perhaps the forgotten green
of a medieval bride's gown, a fertility charm?

The lines, scratched in with palette knife,
these sweeps with stabs of brush are there to sing.
Take off your shoes and listen
to the introspective kora,
here a dab of plangent flute
and a line of the spirits of the gamelan
or mesmerising samba.
Let your centre be stilled
by the echo of plainsong
in a chapel on an island
surrounded by Atlantic waves
the colour of Celtic *glas*
that is both blue and green.

Pauline Plummer

Salad Days

You enjoyed a picnic in the park among buttercups white daisies
Soft lettuce and sweet tomato sandwiched in slices of uncut bread
A brown egg shelled sprinkled with fine salt and white pepper
Your favourite pie, home-made with a brown sugar crust,
Victoria sponge butter icing between layers wrapped in greaseproof:
Chasing puffed up balloons, seeing them wriggle out of sight
Into the blue, beyond the trees never to be seen again.

Today under the awning a Caesar with bacon bits, garlic croutons
Capsicums in paint-box yellow, leaf-green, carmine red
Courgettes from your Gardening Club
Drizzled, snuggled in a sun-dried panini,
Gherkins to *nip the lips*, soothe with a Chardonnay:
For afters lemon sorbet, pistachio and lime cheesecake
A whisked pear and mango smoothie under crushed meringue.

Monica Sharp

Green Glade Sounds

When at first you look you hear a woodland,
your vision muted by the clack of leaves.
But in this place the sound of green deceives
the eye. You listen to an outstretched hand
and grasp at steps to take you from a grand
crescendo and some whining grass that grieves
because its sway's drowned out inside a breeze.
Every wave's abducted by the sea's command.

Ignore the hopeful patch, the beat of blue,
your horizon's plainly deafened by a cloud.
There, did you hear your lips go dry, as dew
torpedoed to the bottom of the earth's bowl? Vowed
to silence by the screaming shrubs do you
yellow out and vanish in the crowd?

Maureen Almond

Jeff Luke

9-5 Part II, 1995

Found objects, elastic bands and tables
© Jeff Luke Estate

Gifted by the Jeff Luke Estate

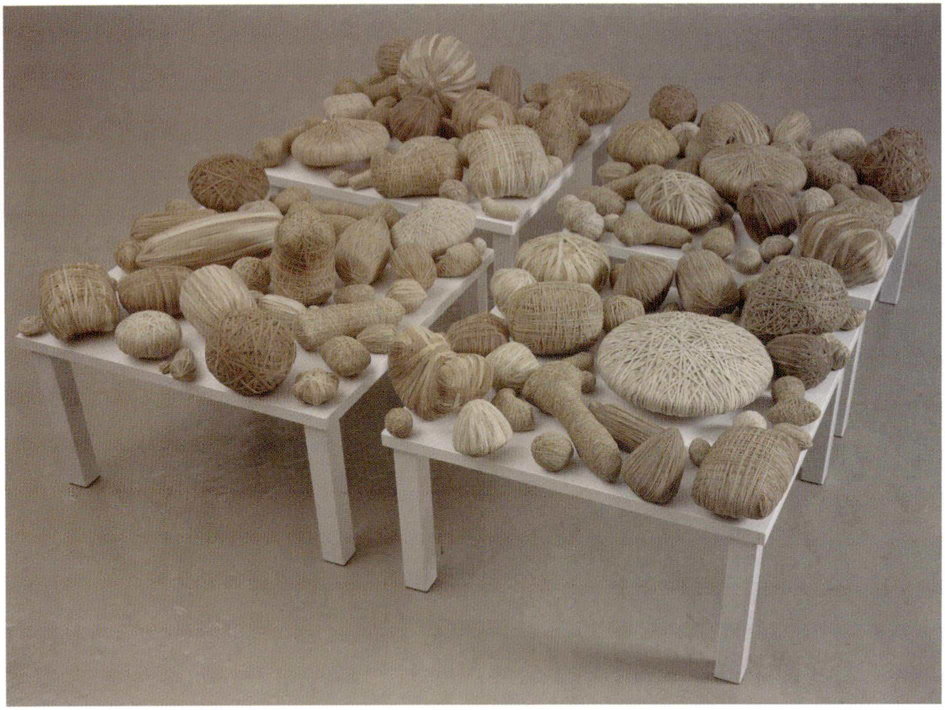

The De-Generation Game

Making shapes out of rubber bands,
What a way to make a living.
You stretched them wide
As your body grew too big for its bed.
Most people leave a will,
You had to be different
But you were always the same.
Running off to London, whilst your friends stayed here,
I always hoped you'd come back
But not like this.
I often wonder what I would do
If I was given a year to live.
Would I shave my head, plant a tree,
Make sure your dad found someone else?
When you get old, your nose and ears keep growing
Whilst the rest shrinks into dust.
At 33 you just kept growing
and mummified things you didn't think I'd miss.
I want to feel the soft rubber,
To stroke the white dust
That looks like cradle-cap,
To see if I can smell you
Amongst the rubbery tang.
My carriage clock is somewhere here,
Ticking away, going on without me,
As I go on without you.

Natalie Boxall

Christmas Day

Perfect little parcels,
ripe with waiting –
bound together
by their sameness –
a family now.
When something does not break
it can look like love.
We all smile
we just can't snap out of it.

*Mum's mouth is so tight
her lips have disappeared
but the apple of her chin
it's twitching
under a blanket of skin.*

*I am listening, I am listening now
– there is a sound –
it is somewhere between
a swallow and
[you just might feel]
a sharp pin prick.
It's a sound like forgetting
and earth falling.*

On Christmas Eve
some things are bound up tight,
tucked in –
beyond the grasp of little fingers
which can't sleep.

On Christmas Day
they will be taken down
from dark places
but we are only
allowed to run
our finger tip
along the outline
and guess.

It is such a luxury – to break.
I can hold it in
until it's just like breathing – forgetting.
I can hold the line
I can stop it
Stretching out into the memory of its true shape.
Forgetting is good –
it's just like a stitch,
you can wear it off
going round and round
in your slippers.

'It's the quiet ones you need to watch'
because there is always a sometimes –
it starts with a smile in the wrong place.
The breaking itself is so gentle,
it surprises me.
It is too quiet,
so that we do not notice
the parcel in our hands –
the one bound so carefully,
so tightly
with something so like love –
is only the mess left behind.

Carmen Thompson

Ceal Floyer

Detail from **Ink on Paper, 2001**

Felt tip pen on blotting paper
© Ceal Floyer

Photography Gilmar Ribeiro g2
Presented by the Contemporary Art Society, 2003, purchased with a grant from Arts Council England with funding from the National Lottery

Ink on Paper

They are right up there on the wall
Waiting for me.
Right up there, as I walk through the door:
Twelve dots; different sizes, different colours,
All neatly centred on their slides,
Dominating their space like small suns.
A million miles away
A nurse drops a tray of instruments,
And for a moment
It seems they are coming at me,
Trying to pierce the glass.

He starts to explain and points with his finger,
Taking me through it frame by frame.
'It's the fuzzy ones,' he says,
Giving the reds particular attention,
'They are the problem.'
I say 'Oh' in a voice that makes no sense
And he says, 'We'd like you in a.s.a.p.'
And I say, 'Well, when would that be?'
A pause. 'Tomorrow?'
And I say 'Oh' in a voice that makes no sense.

Geoff Strange

Setting Out Our Stall

We are available for purchase today.
We are available in a variety of colours.
Singles, pairs and multiples available for purchase.
We are fully adjustable and can co-ordinate any fur or scale combination.

We are twelve inner sleeves from forgotten album covers,
twelve unusual months,
twelve sneaky cultures growing on Petrie dishes,
twelve killer cocktails,
twelve designer breasts,
twelve prototypes for false monster eyes,
twelve tooth-rotting sweets,
twelve disturbing dreams,
twelve humming-bird snares.
Twelve smears of twelve new diseases,
we burst through litmus twelve times.

Our names are:

Brown, darkness within a lighter circle
Red, pink middle, green blobs spreading
Bright pink, red centre scattered wide
Orange hot pink centre
Electric blue singing, pucker-paper
Royal blue, rock pool fringing
Gold and a pink aura
Egg yolk yellow
Firm smaller green with a blue aura
Bigger nucleus with a shifted blue aura
Purple frilly psychedelic anemone
Shades of black axolotl gills

Play with us. Each one of us.
We shall unfold in twelve different ways.
You will open and absorb us.
You will not be disappointed.

Diane Cockburn

L.S. Lowry

The Old Town Hall and St. Hilda's Church, 1959

Oil on canvas
©The Estate of L. S. Lowry, 2007

Photography Gilmar Ribeiro, g2

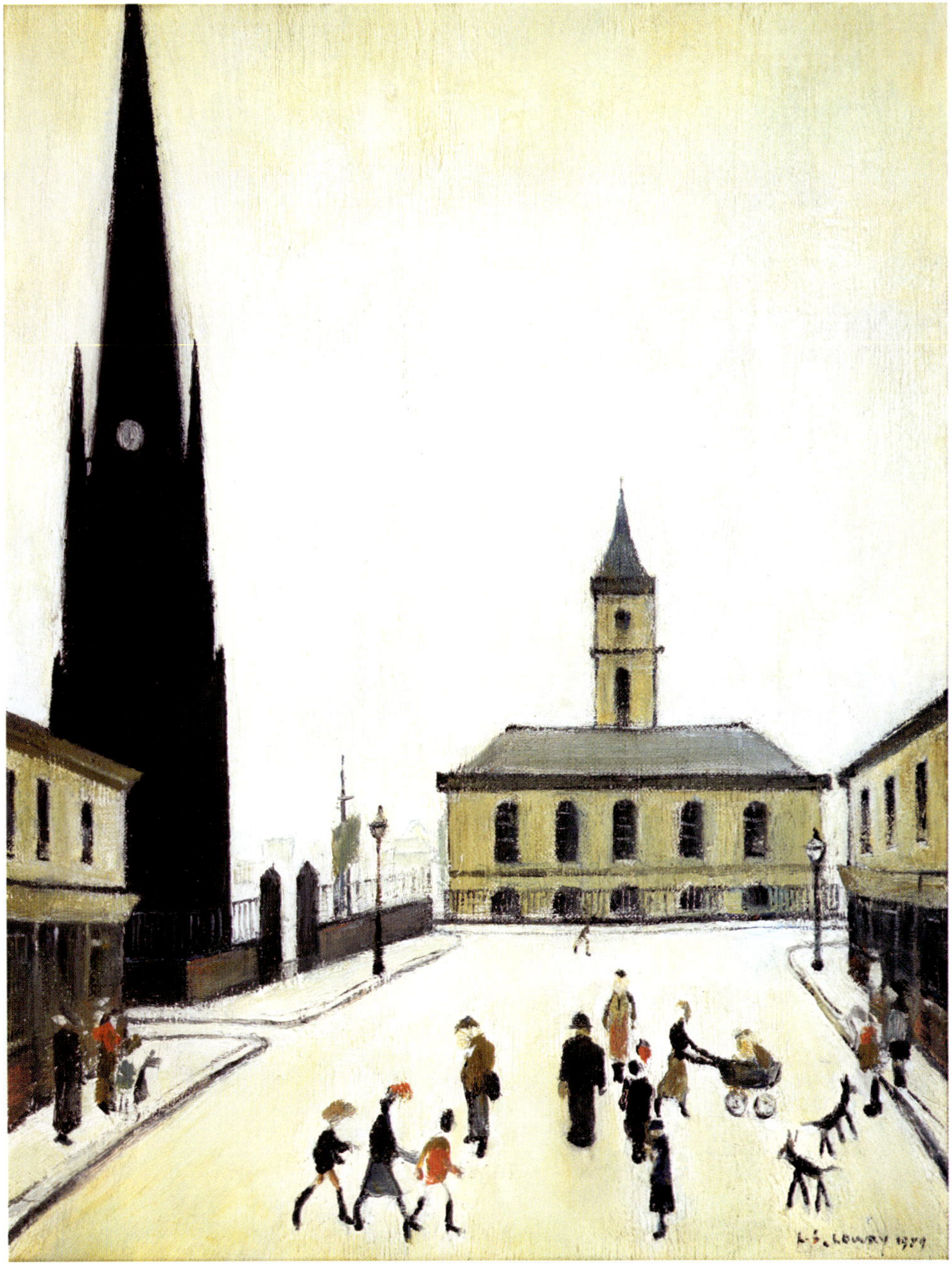
L.S. LOWRY 1959

The Old Town Hall

The small song of a lonely man fills the picture.
That's him in the middle of the street,
Hands in pockets, doing nothing in particular.
Just staring.
People eddy about him, the world flows by,
And he sings of a black church, a road
Going nowhere, an empty sky.

Geoff Strange

The Old Town Hall and St Hilda's Church

Every morning Uncle Jack would cycle by
To his work on the paddle tug *John L. Amos*
Moored at a jetty near the Transporter Bridge.
His clipped trouser legs pushing pedals round
Riding down the street towards the river.
Slung over his shoulder his old khaki gas mask case
Containing his bait box and billy can.
He was the lone cyclist just out of picture
Cycling towards the dog walkers, pram pusher,
Mother escorting children to school, gossipers on the pavement.
He nodded as he passed the soot-grimed spire of St Hilda's
Soaring heavenwards for, although he was chapel, he loved God.
Towards the old Town Hall with its arched windows,
Its tower a symbol of authority and municipality.
Its proud motto *ERIMUS – We Shall Be*, a fitting aspiration
By the founding fathers for their infant Hercules, *IRONOPOLIS*.
Shift over, Uncle Jack would cycle slowly by
On his way home to Outram Street.

Keith Porritt

Ex Cathedra

It isn't in the picture, the perfume – Hinton's Noted Teas being blended, infusing wooden rafters, marrying obscure spices. Roasting coffees, invigorating powdery herbs. Faint hints of robust tar and rope wafting from the Docks.

They're not in the picture, silver chutes sultanas cascaded down; turbaned girls catching currants in transparent bags.

'After a bit', they told me, 'you can't smell it. Them that works here don't know it's there.' Blessed on rare visits to Dad's office – a crow's nest above crates of oranges bought at dawn from ships on the quay – the magic didn't blunt in me.

The stick children have different tales. Would they tell me about their different images in the same streets round the old Cathedral? Would they marble mine like sharp lemons infiltrating bland whiffs of custard powder? If I could step into the picture, could we create together a tapestry unsullied by stagnant memory and untainted by inorganic hope? I'd tell the stiff figures about statues inside the huge grime of the blackened church, tiny niches kept immaculate by unpaid pensioners; the Children's Corner an old gypsy mended hymn books in with gleaming tape; jam jars holding wild flowers from ashy crevices on slag-heaps; the still slant of sun alive with pirouetting dust and rainbow fluff. How strange it was, the vaulted emptiness my mother led me about in our infrequent ventures Over The Border, the rural quietude between molten steel and ships' hooters.

It isn't in the picture, the other perfume – oil on hands; tentative maps of townscapes where holy incense on wine-dipped bread embraces aromas of wholegrain flour, meets the woody smell of apples and tea-chests in the seamless robe of Christ.

Norah Hill

Ian Macdonald

Broken Nose, 1975

Silver bromide print
© Ian Macdonald

Photography Gilmar Ribeiro, g2
Acquisition supported by the V&A Purchase Grant Fund

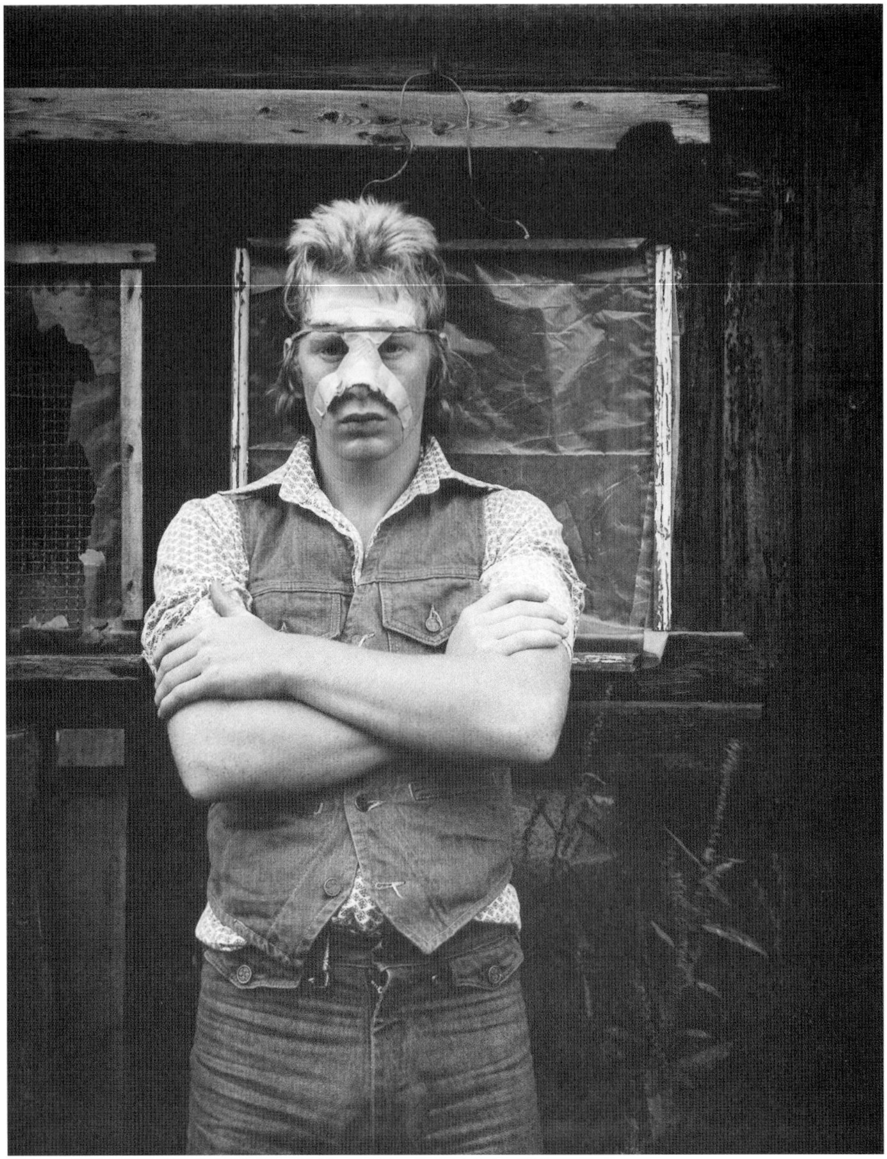

Blooding the Enemy

The pig king has entered my classroom
late   as usual.
He's been fighting again.

And time stops as I drink him in,
savour his faint odour
of stale sweat/pigeon shit, under the *Brût*.

Outside the time-shift,
the rest smoulder –
ham-hand fingers fused into trotters,

solid-hunched, grunting –
these dark lords. I have nothing they want,
nothing to give them.

They know

it's my first year of teaching, know
I'm no Ursula Brangwen,
know

I didn't show who was boss
in the beginning – wearing those mini-skirts,
asking for trouble –

they smell my fear,
the fear of their victim,
and every week   they are waiting.

The pig king strolls to his desk,
stands, square-shouldered, to face me,
his lived-in jeans, zip straining,

shirt-sleeves rolled up to his biceps,
warrior's arms coated in bristle;
a small scar on his wedding-finger knuckle,

cruel stare FULL-ON, mouth so kissable,
daring me.
        'Why are you late? Where's your homework?'

He has my measure,
hands me a photo of himself at the door of his kingdom
'Fancy a visit   Miss?

You know you want to.'

Marilyn Longstaff

You Should've Seen the Other Fellow

I was ready to hide in the allotments
'til they told me how the crest of my mullet cut
and the plaster cast made a gladiator's helmet

I looked amazing and for weeks I was king round here
a hero could do no wrong everyone wanted to talk
about the fight buy me drinks and the girls were shameless
I'll be careful they'd whisper you've got a mouth just like
Marlon Brando what was I to do I knew it wouldn't last
but ended too soon when they took off the cast my beautiful
Roman nose had gone *effing* retroussé.

Ann O'Neill

Richard Slee

Chicken Legs, 2005

Found metal bin, glazed ceramic
© Richard Slee

Photography Gilmar Ribeiro, g2
Acquired through the Northern Rock Foundation Craft Acquisition Fund

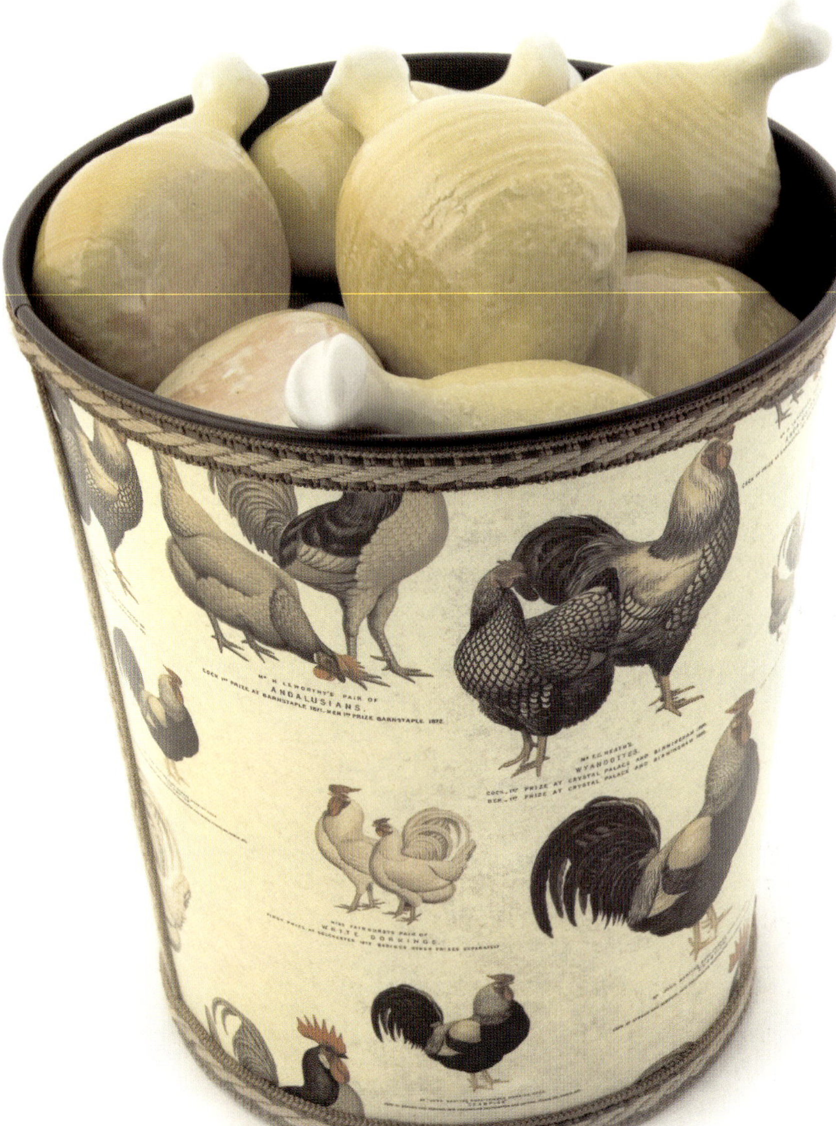
ANDALUSIANS.
WYANDOTTES.

Chicken Legs 2005

Skip the jokes these are not
useful prosthetics cold
oily yellows and veined pinks.

My dad took one and a bit legs
to the grave, the rest was trashed
in a hospital incinerator.

Frank Bird's factory's enough
for a million chicken lives
we eat some at the barbeque.

The smoothed-off stump got sores
in its laced-up leather pouch
tried all sorts, not much use.

You could juggle these thighs
in a ballet of chicken legs
or drop to smithereens.

He walked with a click, a click
that locked the joint
took his weight the next yard.

You stand here, weigh them up
like Marks and Spencer's
free-range big value packs.

Don't their birds have good lives
and he couldn't dance OK
but got around click click.

Long division sums
one flesh, fragmented trajectories
the awkwardness of resurrection.

Some rich Medici kept
a saint's bone in a golden box
you can believe in chicken legs.

Gordon Hodgeon

Chuckalishas

Wanna piece of chuckalishas leg?
Grab a snazzed-up KFC
Limited edition,
Take the whole family home,
Brother, mother, sister, father,
And feast.
Count the feathers on the family album pics
Emblazoned just for you.
See if you can spot me,
The white one with the trill.
Don't forget to cough up the china,
Not fried but fired,
Not greasy but glazed,
Just love that crunching china chuckalishas taste.

Katie Metcalfe

Frank Auerbach

Seated Figure, 1973

Oil on board
© *Frank Auerbach*

Photography Gilmar Ribeiro, g2

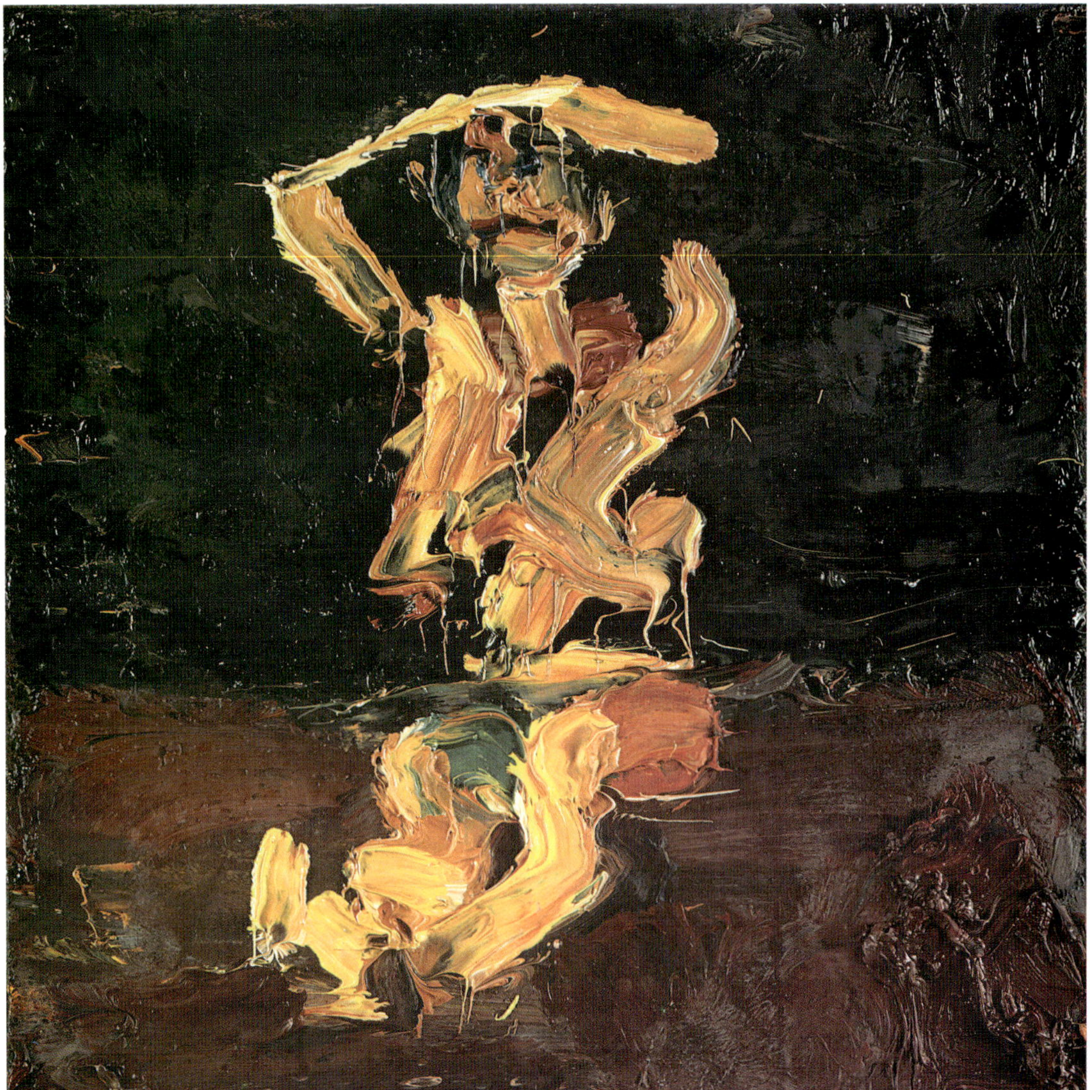

Seated Figure

It's been a good night when you come home
still in tune with the air around you like the holes
in your tin whistle; still spinnin' from the shiver
of pipes and jiggin'n'reelin' limbs loose and free
fall into a chair, kick off the hard shoes, come apart
at the seams

and dream you're a windmill man, a weather-vane
a manikin, a novelty in clockwork orange
dangling from a hook in a tent at the summer-fair
or enjoying a brew with mates on the top floor
better than arthritic under an MRI.

Monica Sharp

Chair

A broken chair
leant against the allotment shed
casts its own row of shadows.

A widow will read them
in a different way to the child
who will see a line of animals,
waves rolling across the bay,
the gentle slopes of Grandad's sheets
before he left that Wednesday night
to visit somebody whose name,
always whispered,
sounded as if it started with a J –
like jelly and Grandad's geraniums.

There are times even a child knows
that some questions
must remain inside their head.

The plot grows thicker than a jungle.
There will be a season
when a broken chair,
propped against the leaning shed,
takes root, comes into leaf. Possibly
a flower or two.

Pat Borthwick

Auerbach's Figure

This god, bored with the ponderous,
heavy moving beasts of heretofore,
dreamed a new amusement
for future wet sixth day afternoons.

Sick of this dark noisome goo
poked a finger in to see what it was about
drawing a prototype, in vivid colours, of a two-legged kind
a figure with movement.

It's not quite free, though no strings are seen.
It comes at you out of this morass
of dark unconsciousness, a bright idea
a kingfisher flash of what might be.

Anne Hine

Henri Gaudier-Brzeska
Wrestlers, 1913

Relief, (Herculite)

Photography Gilmar Ribeiro, g2

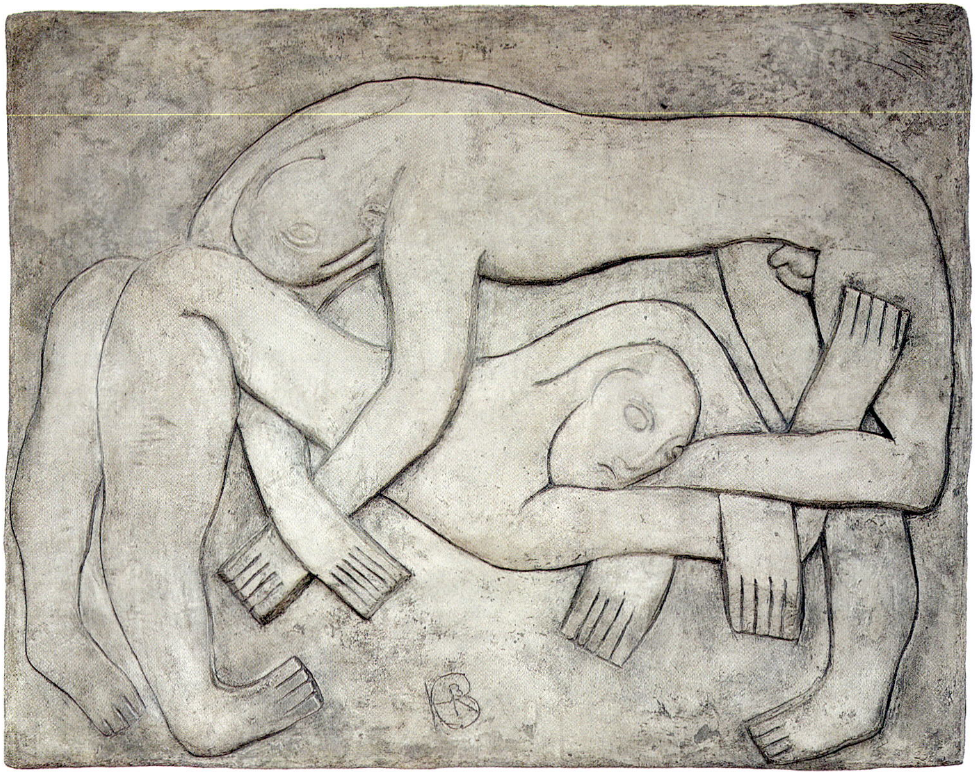

The Wrestling

They used to like to watch the wrestling
on Saturday's TV, the thwap of thigh
on canvas, in black and white, the twist,
the neck-hold, the grunt, the shriek as love cry
of submission – manly chest on manly chest,
shammed suffering in the muscled pecs,
flesh and intimate without the mortal sin.
Home was thick with fights – boxing
with shared gloves – mum and dad went a round
or two. I wonder if she thought of an old flame
who'd wrestled a bear to the ground
in Toxteth, skinned it and given her the coat.
I might've had Mad Kelly as a surname
and seized life less tightly by the throat.

Pauline Plummer

Wrestlers

Sleepy wrestlers,
they've fought so long
they have become lovers.
Clasping each other's bodies,
wrapped in flesh,
smooth and greased,
their faces conceal their delight.
For men cannot love in 1914,
only fight.

Biblical denial of what you feel;
to be this close to another man.
Smell his odour.
Hold him.
Enough for now,
a memory for later.

Joseph S. Kelley

Getting There in Spite Of

Always fighting, neither strong enough to win,
the daily pattern from when they could stand,
shove and unbalance one another. Each twin
was his brother's mirror. Who'd have planned

this halving at the start, tangle in the womb,
the having to share it all, the fierce demand
for attention from their trodden-down mum?
No wonder they were all set to be drowned

those sons of Mars whose future would be Rome.
Mine had no excuse; admittedly the sound
of despair, wolf-like, might echo from our home:
both needed to be the one laurel-crowned.

No fight to the death (it wasn't that long ago)
like Jove's sons patterning the night sky.
Mine grew out of win or lose; best mates now,
quite lovable really. Stars in my sky.

Jo Heather

Colin Pearson

Large Winged Vessel, 1982

Thrown and constructed stoneware with manganese glaze
© Estate of Colin Pearson

Photography Gilmar Ribeiro, g2

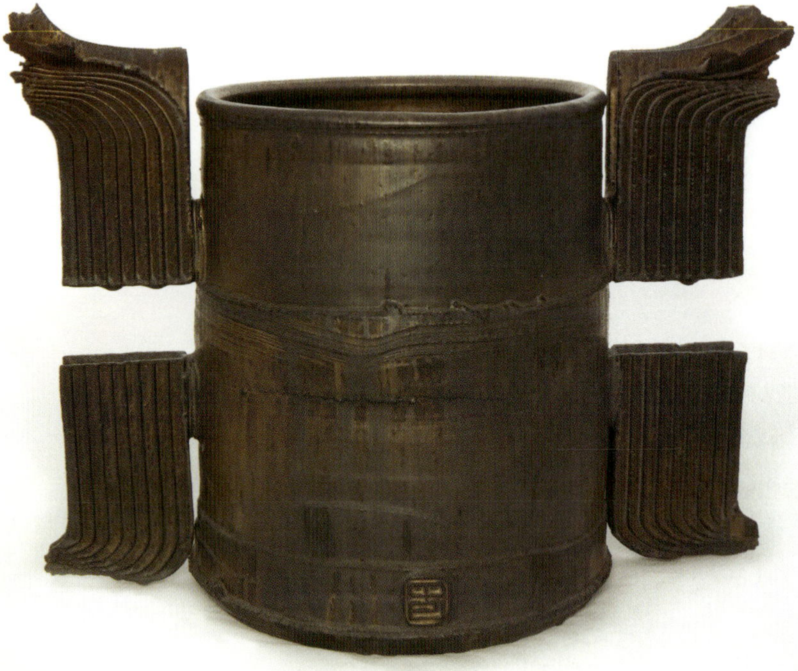

Large Winged Vessel

Woden, Wotan, Wodan, Odin,
father of the gods
let me drink deep
from the large winged vessel.
Forged in the darkest smithy,
finely chased
with bloodrunes and spiritsong,
receptacle of wisdom.
With thought and memory
may the ravens carry tidings
of my humble plea,
as I offer up incense and prayers.
Judge me worthy
to drink deep
blood and honey
the mead of inspiration.
Lord of sewing and salting,
shield and spear,
father of all gods
let me share this cup.
Let me drink deep
from the large winged vessel.
Woden, Wotan, Wodan, Odin,
god of poets
hear my call.

Jon Glasper

Large Winged Vessel

You found me six feet down
trowels itching for skin:
two chipped curves of bones
brushed clean, out into sun.

Revealed this baked clay ring
from the dirt, remembered song
of an evil time, blew my strong
horn, each bruised bone a wing.

In air I squat, in light, coiled heavy
as heaviest artillery,
immune and monstrous bee,
thick-set on slaughter: 'What I do is me.'

Will winged vessel fly or speak,
bleed for you? You might break
my silence, prove your scholastic
cunning, get your frost to crack

glazed hide where no nerve lives.
It is not that I am brave
to withstand you, not that I love
death. I was born to this in the hive.

Gordon Hodgeon

The One

Illustrious prince, my hero.
I can't stop gazing at you,
so bronzed and powerful.
True your hands are bony fins
and your feet are froggy
but you're no slippery thing from a pond.
You're not as old as you look.

If I were a match girl, milkmaid,
emperor's daughter
I could ping open your sealed box.
You'll be warm and tweedy to my touch,
smell of aired shirts, heather, pinewoods.
If I kiss you
feathered arms will hold me close.

Jo Heather

Edward Burra

The Market, 1967

Ink and felt tip on paper
Courtesy of Edward Burra Estate c/o Lefevre Fine Art, London

Photography Gilmar Ribeiro, g2

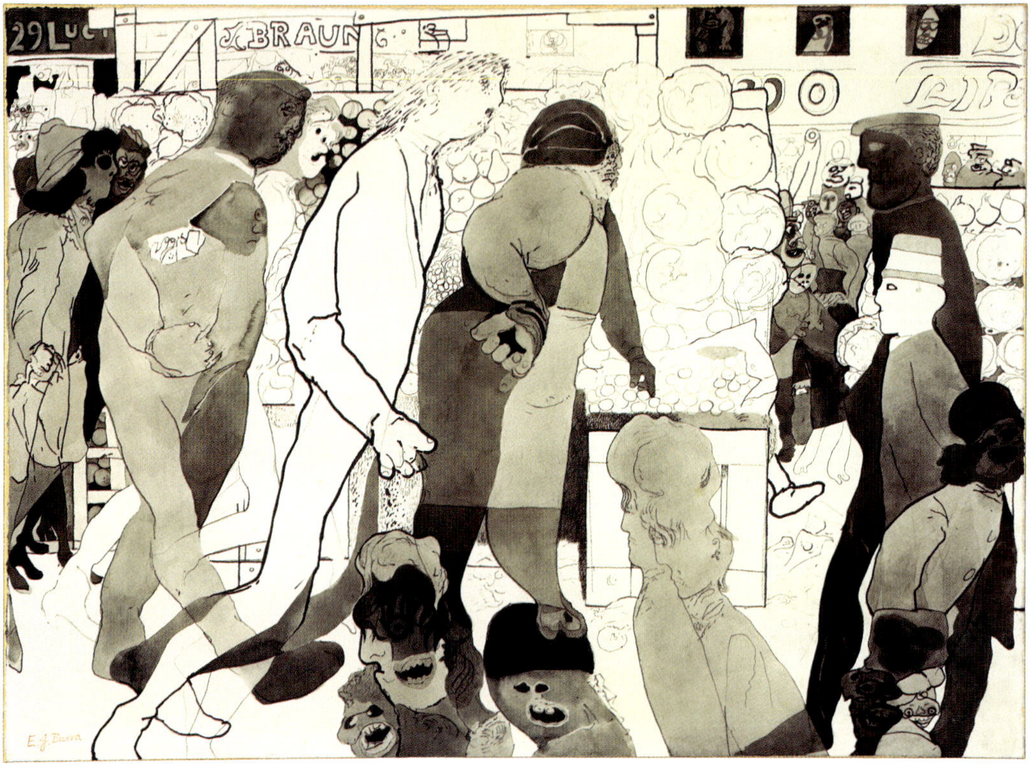
BRAUN

Don' Mek Me

Ah don' like it
Ah don' like it one bit
Mama jes give me two dollar piece
her ole string bag and say
Lard dis girl
sent fi try mi pashunce

She don' see dem carrot girls
wid yellah teef and bully lip
how dem bad mouth me
all di way to market

Today dey wid dey mudda
in her wilty lettuce hat
so di carrots ain' misbehavin'
dem snarl like turnip lantern
at Halloween

Mi dodge pinch-botty man, trip
over ankle bones of skelly man
run helter-pelter to back of queue
Mi heart bump thump
in time wid ole Ma Johnson
She bump thump her fist on stall
Plantain Eyes tried to pass her trickster dollar!
Her biceps is butternut squash
You could lick dem wid a rolling pin
and it brek in two. She bad ass him
all de way dung 29th and it me nex!

Mi look down. Ma's legs is
purple eggplant squeezed
in old potato shoes. She fill mi bag
wid fat yam feet, celery legs
cabbage belly, warty fingers
cauliflower brains, melon head

Ah don' like it
Ah don' like it one bit
and mi bag heavy heavy
Mama will say, *Where you bin
'til now? Di pot boil dry – tcha!
Lard dis girl!*

Annie Wright

The Capital of Cabbage-Land

It's ruled by a man who's not all there,
smeared out inside his outline, head
blurred at the edges, like a slugged potato
eaten away inside. Half of him's gone,
but his right hand has extra fingers –
he's the ringmaster cracking his hidden whip
to bring a film of decay over everything.

Whose head is that, tucked under the dark man's arm?
Is that a child or a dog, just out of view?
It will have to fend for itself.
And that foot is not mine. I would leave it there.
I will not enter this world, not mix
with these cabbage heads and spuds of fists,
cauliflower ears, forked carrots, potatoes eyeing me up.
Their gaping mouths with blackened teeth
are turnip lanterns whose candles have gone out.

I was here, once, in a dream,
was kissed by a man with a rotting coconut head
that my fingers sank into as I pushed him away.
He would know me again. I will not come back
to this place of blight and blear,
to compost down into what dark gravesoil.

Joanna Boulter

Don't you find

        your friends: some opaque, some transparent?

Don't you find as you get older
        the grim reaper in a hoodie, looking into your window?

Don't you find as you get older you start seeing
        RIP on shop signs that once read *Lips?*

'Don't you find as you get older you start seeing through everything?'
                                                     Don't you find?

Marilyn Longstaff

CONTRIBUTORS

Maureen Almond's published work includes: *Hot* (1997: Mudfog Press) *Tailor Tacks* (1999: Mudfog Press), *Oyster Baby,* (2002: Biscuit Publishing), *The Works* (2004: Biscuit Publishing) and *Tongues in Trees* (2005: New Writing North). Maureen is a research student at the University of Newcastle where she is studying the poetry of Roman poet Horace and working on her fifth collection.

Pat Borthwick trained in visual art. She worked as a ceramic sculptor and often drew inspiration from the ceramic collection that is now installed in mima. She has full length collections of poetry published by Littlewood Arc, Mudfog and Templar and has won many prizes. She was awarded an International Hawthornden Fellowship in 2003.

Joanna Boulter is half of Darlington's Arrowhead Press. She has had 3 poetry pamphlets published, and several competition successes including first prize in the 2003 Poetry London competition. Her first full collection, *Twenty Four Preludes and Fugues on Dmitri Shostakovich* (Arc Publications) was recently short-listed for the Felix Dennis Forward Best First Collection prize.

Natalie Boxall is from Middlesbrough and works as a BBC journalist. She is a regular contributor to *The Guardian* and *Plan B* magazine, plays for the Middlesbrough Milk Rollers rollerderby team and likes to spend time in Central Library, mima and Albert Park. She is currently writing her first novel and has a Mudfog mentorship with Pat Borthwick.

Jo Colley has lived in the region since 1974. Her day job is as a writer of educational software. Her short stories have been runners up in the Sid Chaplin Awards and in 2007 she received a Northern Promise Award to support a new collection. Jo has a new book of poems from Salt, *Weeping for the Lovely Phantoms*. She has performed at events in the UK and Finland, is a co-ordinator for Colpitts Poets and ran Hydrogen Jukebox in Darlington.

Diane Cockburn is originally from Northern Ireland. Vane Women Press published her first collection *Under Surveillance* in 1999. Later invited to become a Vane Woman, she has never looked back! Her work appears in a variety of poetry and prose anthologies, including *Discoverers* (Mudfog Press), *Writing on Water* (Ragged Raven Press) and *Skin* (Route-online Byteback Books).

Jon Glasper was born in Middlesbrough. He currently works in a bookshop. His work has appeared in such diverse magazines as *Kenaz*, *Out*, *The Crack* and *Fly me to the moon*. He is currently working on a historical novel and is a regular performer at poetry events in the region.

Jo Heather has been writing poetry for the past ten years or so since her retirement from Mental Health Social Work, taking inspiration from the surroundings of her home in the North Yorks. Moors. She has had one pamphlet, *Gold*, published by Mudfog and recently reissued.

Norah Hill was born in Middlesbrough in 1945. Her poems have appeared in *Stand* and *PN Review* and she has published *Of Many-Coloured Glass* (Paranoia Press, 1992), *Over the Border* (Mudfog, 1998) and *Like* (Middlesbrough Poet Laureate, Mudfog 2002). Norah now works as a creative writing tutor with disabled and disadvantaged people.

Anne Hine has lived in the north-east for the last thirty years. She began taking her writing seriously in the 1990s. Her first poetry pamphlet *Dark Matters* was published by Vane Women Press in 2001. She has work in several anthologies: *Smelter*, *Northern Grit*, *Re-writing the Map* and *Gabriel*.

Gordon Hodgeon has published three collections including *Winter Breaks* (Smokestack Books, 2006). Recent work has also appeared in *The Wilds* (Ek Zuban, 2007), *Speaking English* (Five Leaves, 2007) and *North by North-East* (Iron Press, 2006). He won the Mirehouse Poetry Prize in 2004 and 2007.

Joseph S. Kelley has been writing poetry ever since he wrote a poem to a girl which was enough to convince her to marry him. Four years later Joe and his wife Claire now have two children, Esme and Elwood, and live happily in Darlington. Claire is still encouraging him to write more.

Marilyn Longstaff lives in Darlington; member of Vane Women, the writing, performing and publishing collective; Arts Council 'Northern Promise Award' (2003); published in a range of magazines, in anthologies, and on the web; first pamphlet *Puritan Games* (Vane Women Press, 2001); full collection, *Sitting Among the Hoppers* (Arrowhead Press, 2004). At the moment, she is trying to put together a new collection called *Raiment*.

Katie Metcalfe is a writer and survivor. Works include two published books, various poems, articles and short stories in print. Current projects include two novels, a book of poetry, obtaining a degree in Creative Writing at the University of Cumbria, promoting awareness about anorexia nervosa and writing to stay sane.

Sheila Nichols is published in *Glassblowing* (Mudfog, 2001), *The Ticking Crocodile* (Blinking Eye Publishing, 2004). She won second prize in the Summer Academy 2000 Poetry competition and her collection, Plotting the Graph, was highly commended in the New Writer poetry competition 2006. Mudfog pamphlets are *Nice Words*, 1997, *The Improvements*, 2005.

Ann O'Neill was born in 1936. She has had a pamphlet, *Quicksteps*, published by Mudfog, 1994, and poems included in the following anthologies: *Breathless* (Writearound, 1994), *A Hole Like That* (Scratch, 1994), *Throughroutes* with Mollie Hill and Molly Maughan (Mudfog, 1999), *Smelter* (Mudfog, 2003), *The Poetry Cure* (Bloodaxe, 2005) and a first collection, *The Sugar Factory* (Diamond Twig, 2004).

Pauline Plummer has two full collections and two collaborations with an artist - most recently *Bamako to Timbuktu,* published for an exhibition at The Biscuit Factory in Newcastle. Her short stories are published in anthologies e.g. *Newcastle Stories* (Comma Press). She has taught creative writing for Northumbria and Sierra Leone Universities, in Greece and in schools, prisons and community centres.

Keith Porritt took up writing on his retirement. His Mudfog pamphlet, *High Level Apprentice*, was published in 2005. He has also had work published by Blinking Eye, Thwengway Press and several magazines. A keen walker with his wife in earlier years, he hopes to publish poetic narratives on the Cleveland Way and the Coast-to-Coast Walk. He is interested in the use of technical and scientific language in his poetry.

Monica Sharp, as well as having poems published in several anthologies, enjoys writing short stories, one of which has been accepted by Dogeater. A long-term project is writing the stories of three exceptional women who had to leave Cornwall and settle in the North East: her great grandmother, grandmother and mother with a generous sprinkle of Irish here and there.

Adrienne Silcock's first novel *Vermin* (Flambard) was published in 2000. Her poetry has appeared in *Other Poetry*, *Psychopoetica* and *Miracles and Clockwork* (Other Poetry Editions, 2005). She was involved in the *Voices of Women* performance poetry project in conjunction with *Wicked Words Poetry*, Leeds, and won the 1998 Old Meeting House play-writing competition.

Geoff Strange has lived on Teesside for almost thirty years and the history and landscape beauty of the North East have become recurring themes in his poetry. He has produced a poetry pamphlet, *Words on a Map,* and contributed to a number of anthologies, all published by Mudfog Press.

Carmen Thompson's poetry is dominated by themes of childhood, relationships, nature and home. She likes to unravel the detail in a single moment or gesture. She gained her MA in English in 2000 and since then has taught English and Creative Writing. She has written and performed for *The Writers' Café* and *Kenaz* and her work has appeared in the *Redcar Writers Anthology* and *Teesway 199*.

Annie Wright's first full collection, *Redemption Songs*, came out in 2003 from Arrowhead Press. Her pamphlet, *Including Sex*, was published by the Bay Press in 1995 and she was included in the Iron Press anthology *North By North-East* in 2006. She is a member of Vane Women and edits work for their press.